A Dragon in a Wagon

A book about ways to travel

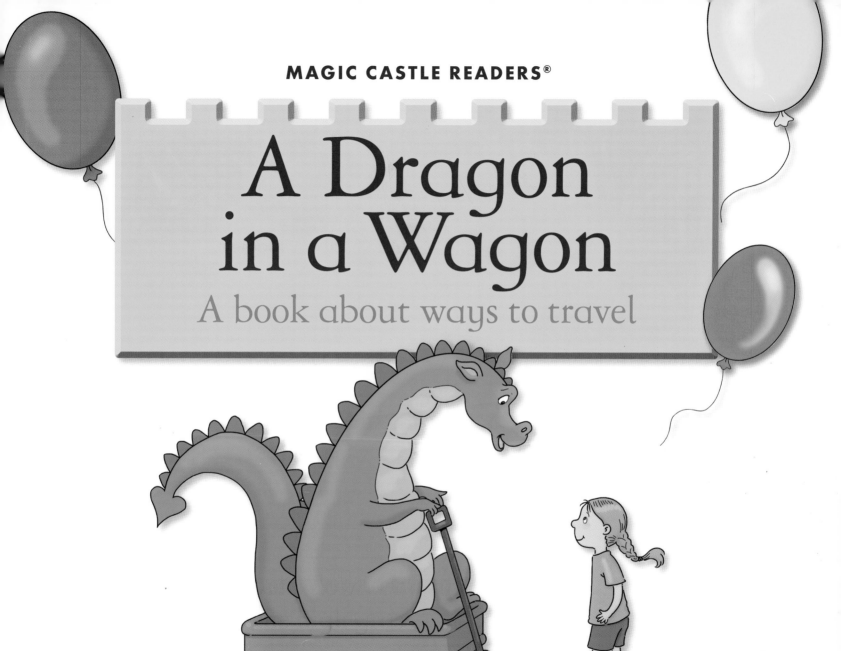

BY JANE BELK MONCURE • ILLUSTRATED BY DANA REGAN

The Child's World

Published by The Child's World®
1980 Lookout Drive • Mankato, MN 56003-1705
800-599-READ • www.childsworld.com

Acknowledgments
The Child's World®: Mary Berendes, Publishing Director
The Design Lab: Design
Jody Jensen Shaffer: Editing

ISBN 9781623235734
LCCN 2013931413

Printed in the United States of America
Mankato, MN
July 2013
PA02177

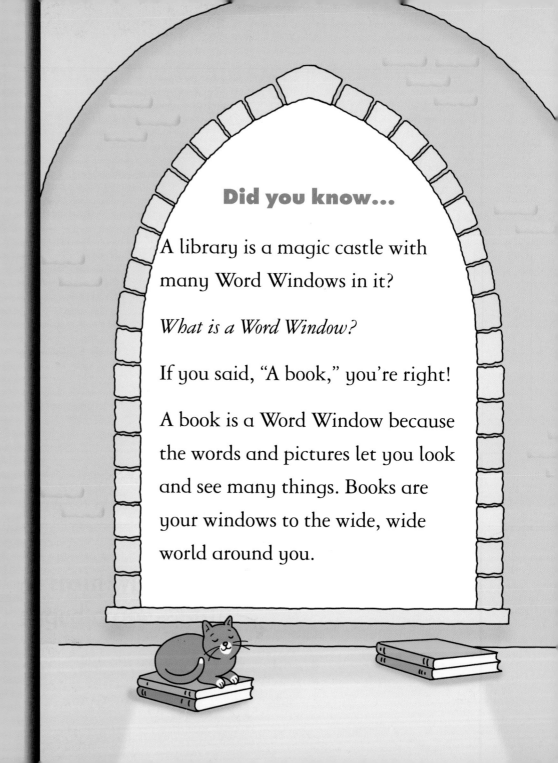

Did you know...

A library is a magic castle with many Word Windows in it?

What is a Word Window?

If you said, "A book," you're right!

A book is a Word Window because the words and pictures let you look and see many things. Books are your windows to the wide, wide world around you.

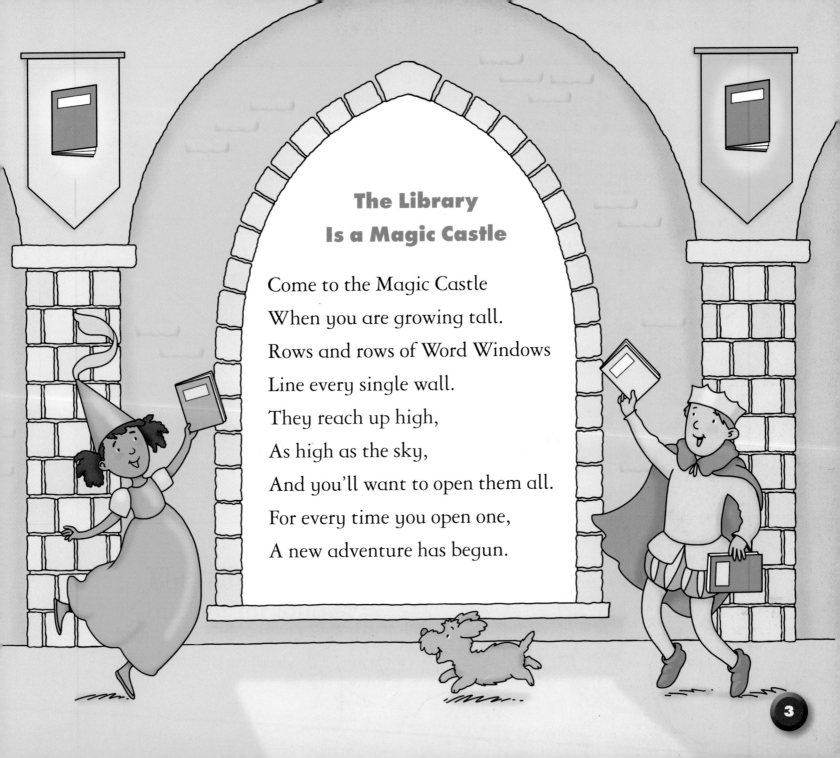

The Library
Is a Magic Castle

Come to the Magic Castle
When you are growing tall.
Rows and rows of Word Windows
Line every single wall.
They reach up high,
As high as the sky,
And you'll want to open them all.
For every time you open one,
A new adventure has begun.

Megan opens a Word Window.
Guess what she sees.

A dragon in a wagon.
"Hi," says the dragon. "Let's go for a ride."

"Good idea," says Megan. She hops inside.

But the wagon does not go very far.

Megan and the dragon hop into a car.

But the car will not go.

They hop on a bus with a horse
and a hippopotamus.

But the bus will not go.

They jump into a boat with a dog,
three cats, and a billy goat.

But the boat will not float.

They hop on a sled with a moose who has
five funny mice on his head.

But the sled will not go.

They jump on a truck with a cow,
three pigs, a hen, and a duck.

But the truck will not go.

They hop on a train with an elephant
and a long-legged crane.

But the train will not go.

It starts to rain. So they hop off the train
and step into a plane.

But the plane will not fly.

So they float in the sky.

"Where are you going?" asks a bird flying by.

"I don't know," says Megan,
"but we'll be there soon."

As soon as they land, they find a balloon.

"Whee!" says the dragon. "Let's fly to the moon!
Let's keep going and fly to a star!"

"Oh no," says Megan, "I will not go that far.
I think we should stop. Do you see where we are?"

Megan waves to a clown and a girl on a swing.

Then the dragon finds his favorite thing.

"Come along!" says the dragon as he rides away.

"No, thank you," says Megan. "No more rides
today. Good-bye, dragon in a wagon."

Questions and Activities
(Write your answers on a sheet of paper.)

1. In one sentence, tell what this book is about.
   What details does the author use to tell the story?

2. Did this story have any words you don't know?
   How can you find out what they mean??

3. Describe Megan and the dragon.
   Write two things about each character.

4. Why did Megan not want to fly to the moon?
   How do you know?

5. Why did Megan and the dragon get off the train?
   Why do they keep changing rides?